In the Realm of Pleasure represents a major revision of current feminist-psychoanalytic theories of film pleasure and sexual difference. Gaylyn Studlar's close textual analysis of the six Paramount studio films directed by Josef von Sternberg and starring Marlene Dietrich probes the source of their visual and psychological complexity. Addressing questions of visual and narrative style in *Morocco, Blonde Venus, Dishonored, Shanghai Express, The Scarlet Empress,* and *The Devil Is a Woman,* she offers a radical countertheory to Lacanian and Freudian approaches to film response and the representation of gender.

Borrowing from Gilles Deleuze's psychoanalytic-literary approach to the novels of Leopold von Sacher-Masoch, the namesake of masochism, and modern object-relations theory, Studlar defines masochism as a mother-centered, pre-Oedipal phenomenon. Like Deleuze, she shows how masochism extends beyond the purely clinical realm into the arena of artistic form, language, and production of pleasure through a text. In films the "masochistic aesthetic" is often characterized by the presence of a female who serves as the authoritative object of male masochistic desire within a sensualized atmosphere of diffuse sexuality. Her examination of the von Sternberg/Dietrich American collaborations shows how these films, with the mother figure embodied in the alluring yet androgynous Marlene Dietrich, offer a key for understanding the masochistic aesthetic in film.

According to Studlar, masochism is an overlooked aspect of cinematic pleasure that demands the reconsideration of classical Hollywood film's appeal to and representation of gender difference. She argues that masochism's broader significance to film study lies in the similarities between the structures of the perversion and those of the cinematic apparatus as a dream screen reviving archaic visual pleasures for both male and female spectators.

"Studlar's book makes an original, convincing, and well-researched case for the importance of a 'masochistic aesthetic' in film. Along the way, it also offers an impressive reassessment of the films of Josef von Sternberg."
— Linda Williams, author of *Figures of Desire: A Theory and Analysis of Surrealist Film*

Photo: Mark Wall

GAYLYN STUDLAR is assistant professor of film studies at Emory University.

Mud Show

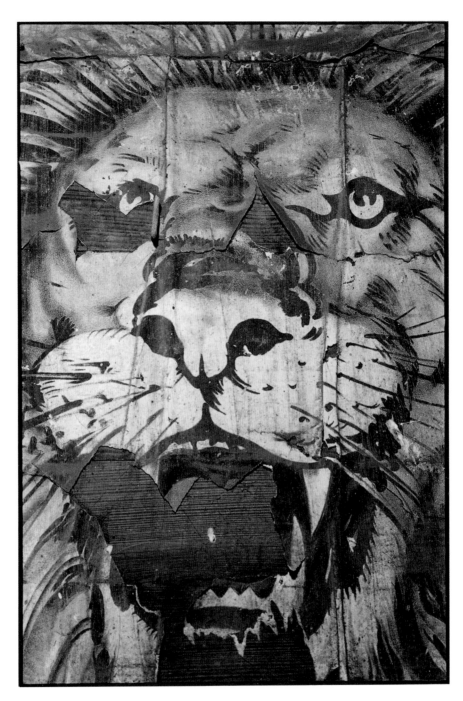

Lion poster, Hugo, Oklahoma,
1985 (Carson & Barnes, winter
quarters).

Mud Show

American Tent Circus Life

Photographs by Edwin Martin

Essay by Don B. Wilmeth

University of New Mexico Press
Albuquerque

Design: Milenda Nan Ok Lee

Library of Congress Cataloging-in-Publication Data

Martin, Edwin, 1943–
  Mud show.

  Bibliography: p.
    1. Circus—United States—History. 2. Circus—
United States—Pictorial works. I. Wilmeth, Don B.
II. Title.
GV1803.M25 1988   791.3′0973 87-19167
ISBN 0-8263-1024-9 (pbk.)

Printed in Japan

Contents

Preface

The lure of the circus is strong, pulling with the attraction of strange animals and mysterious people traveling to exotic places. It is a micro-society of wondrous performers banded together to display death-defying feats.

But underlying the glitter is a hard life, one filled with eighteen-hour work days, usually seven days each week. It is a life in which children struggle with education in the absence of qualified, systematic supervision. It is a business facing sharp increases in insurance and fuel costs as well as stricter regulation. And it is a legacy in transition. In sixty years American transportation went from the horse to jet airline; nuclear-generated electricity replaced gas lights; and communication by word of mouth was supplanted by electronics. As America changed, so has its tent circuses. Like the rest of the country, they too are trying to prepare for the twenty-first century.

These photographs are about such things, about glamour, hardship, tradition, and change. They are also about the rest of us, for the circus continues to be a reflection of its audiences' wildest hopes and deepest dreams.

America's circuses historically played under tents on grass or dirt lots. When it rained, no matter how large or elegant, the troupe became a "mud show." This term can now be used to distinguish such circuses from those playing in indoor arenas, or sticking primarily to paved surfaces. Contemporary mud shows, with mostly American performers, are the spiritual descendants of the American circuses of the past.

Many people have aided in a variety of ways this attempt to compile a portrait of contemporary American tent circus life. First, my photographic education owes much to many. Among the people I am indebted to for helping me think about my work are Marcia Busch-Jones, John Cote, Will Counts, Karen Hanson, Reg Heron, Craig Martin, Fenton Martin, Russell Martin, Shannon Martin, Mitch Morrow, Dave Repp, Dennis Senchuk, Joel Snyder, Carole Thompson, Kendell Turner, George Van Arsdale, Cleve Wilhoit, and Frances Wilhoit.

I also owe a great debt to the generous people who are the subjects of my photographs. They lead lives of hard work in preparation for a few moments of glory. And I am indebted to the trust and generosity of the managers of the circuses I traveled with for aiding my access. These include Geary Byrd of Carson & Barnes Circus, David Rawls of the Al G. Kelly–Miller Brothers Circus, Wayne Franzen of Franzen Brothers Circus, John Pugh of Clyde Beatty–Cole

Brothers Circus, Susie Garden of Toby Tyler Circus, and Doris Earle of Roberts Brothers Circus. I also value the aid given to me by Ben Barkin of The Great Circus Parade. And my special thanks go to Mr. D. R. Miller through whose faith and foresight I was able to begin this work with Carson & Barnes.

—Edwin Martin

Introduction

Don B. Wilmeth

The purpose of this essay is not to attempt in words what Edwin Martin has accomplished so wonderfully through his evocative and almost elegiac photographs of seven of today's typical traveling tent circuses. Indeed, the American circus has always realized that despite flamboyant language and overstatement, perfected over the years by some of mankind's most imaginative and verbally adept press agents, the images of the circus can best be evoked by visual means and not words, even though, unlike these candid but artistically composed photographs, the graphics of the circus have tended to focus on exaggerated claims and the more spectacular displays. Nor, should I add, do I feel in any way capable of accomplishing such a feat. The raison d'être for this volume is the photographic artistry of Edwin Martin, centered on the dying American circus, and each of the photographs represented here—from back-lot portraits of clowns in their more pensive and human moods, to action shots in the center ring juxtaposed next to a weekly religious service in the same venue, to moments of everyday living captured on the lot—can easily stand on its own merits without the need of explanatory paragraphs.

This introduction is not meant to be a scholarly effort; for the circus expert there is nothing new here, though the historical summations and speculative thoughts attempt to refresh memories for the knowledgeable and to provide some basic information and ideas for the neophyte. At best I would like what follows to be a complement to Martin's photographs; in truth, I suspect it is more of a counterpoint, pointing toward the photographs as the centerpiece of this volume.

Specifically what I hope the following pages accomplish is to provide a sense of the tradition and history of the American circus and to explain, at least in part, its age-old appeal, its uniqueness in comparison to the circus of Europe, what makes it a very American institution, and its evolution to what must surely be considered today a hanging-on but a clear decline in quality. My aim is to give those who experience Ed Martin's work some sense of perspective of where these particular circuses fit not only in the long annals and continuum of the American circus but also in the long tradition of artists and their attempts to capture visually this very special live entertainment form and subculture of society, which, though all but vanished from the American scene, continues to fascinate and attract. Although the way of life depicted in this collection has largely been obliterated by the advances of our modern world, the circus world continues to struggle along, providing for those of us who care to partake a vivid and living link with our cultural past. Despite the spectacles possible through computerized magic in the media and the slick and technologically enhanced performances so common today, these circuses also provide good, clean, and often exciting entertainment!

Historical Survey

The modern circus is truly an international art form, depending not on language but on the live exhibition of skilled performances, including the antics of clowns and trained animals presented, usually, within one or more rings surrounded by an audience. The European and Russian form of the circus has tended toward permanency, the one-ring form, and a focus on the individual circus act; in contrast, the uniqueness of the American circus has often been noted as having been associated with mobility, multiple rings, and spectacle. This is still in large measure a real distinction, although as part of the American experience the major circuses have changed over the years as society has changed, and concessions have been made to adapt to current tastes and methods. Even the multiple rings are often something of a deception, for many contemporary three-ring American circuses rarely have more than one ring active at a time. Perhaps the most obvious physical change has been the trend toward performance in venues other than the traditional tent. The most notable exceptions are the type of circuses captured by the camera of Edwin Martin—generally small, sometimes one-ring affairs that still travel many miles playing short dates under the big top. As will be illustrated in this survey, this tradition is one that has been eliminated by America's best-known circus, Ringling Brothers and Barnum & Bailey. As major as this circus is, dominating the American consciousness, however, it should not be the only image of today's American circus, for many smaller towns and cities still see only the smaller, traveling circuses, and even the few larger tented shows, also represented in Martin's photographs, play the truly major cities. These circuses are frequently called mud shows. In the *Language of American Popular Entertainment* (Greenwood Press, 1981) I defined a mud show as follows:

Originally, a circus mud show traveled overland by a horse-drawn wagon, the wheels of which were frequently mired in mud. Prior to 1872, in fact, all circuses were mud shows, and some continued to travel that way until the early 1920s. Later, the term was applied to any circus that traveled overland by wagon, truck, or automobile. Such a show, sometimes called an overland trick or mud op'ry, usually played small towns or the suburbs of large cities. Today, it is a derogatory term used by the large circuses who move by private train to refer to any show not using the luxury of steel rails.

By today's standards, all but Ringling Brothers and Barnum & Bailey could be termed mud shows, although, ironically, most tent show workers and performers consider their circuses the spiritual descendents of the Ringling operation during its big-top heydey and not the antiseptic and almost mechanized show that now plays in permanent arenas. Certainly a mud show today does not mean the circus is small or uncoordinated. Two of the larger contemporary circuses, Carson & Barnes and Clyde Beatty–Cole Brothers, are represented in these photographs, but they too qualify as mud shows by today's standards and cer-

4

tainly in comparison to the enormous operations of the past.

But the mud show as represented by Martin's photographs is only part of a long and rich history and tradition, one that has yet to be definitively told or documented.* Perhaps the full story can never be recorded, for the very nature of the circus—transitory, flamboyant, given to exaggeration and misleading promotion—encourages confusion and imprecision in its telling. Even the names associated with specific circuses lead to unexpected turns and deadends, for the same names have frequently been used by many shows; ownerships frequently changed and names were often transferred to totally different operations. As John and Alice Durant have illustrated in their *Pictorial History of the American Circus* (1957), for example, the name of the Cole Brothers Circus was created by Martin Downs for his show of 1906–8. Later the name was used by at least four others until 1935, when Jess Adkins and Zack Terrell built a new circus with equipment from the Christy and Robbins shows and elsewhere, adopting the name Cole Brothers for their circus. They survived until 1948 when Terrell sold it to Jack Tavlin. Sold again in 1949, the show folded after the 1950 season. However, this was not the end of the name of Cole Brothers, for right up to the present the title has been used in variation by other shows such as King Brothers and Cole Brothers, Famous Cole Circus, and today's Clyde Beatty–Cole Brothers. This pattern has been typical. Adding to this difficulty is the fact that of the undocumented hundreds of circuses

*See Note on Sources at the end of the essay.

that have existed in the United States, many disappeared almost as soon as they were conceived. Yet the dozens that survived, and even those that lasted for only a brief time, carved out a rich circus history. According to some estimates, in the course of the circus's history (through the 1950s), there have been in the United States, Canada, and Mexico since 1771 over 1,100 circuses and menageries. I suspect the number is considerably higher, especially if the very small operations that have existed, even though briefly, over the past thirty years were added to this estimate.

Even the origin of our circus is veiled in mystery and conjecture, going back certainly to the wandering jugglers, tumblers, and animal trainers entertaining people before recorded history. We can begin to see aspects of the modern circus in some of the activities found in the English fairs of the seventeenth and eighteenth centuries. One major appeal of the English fair, which can also be considered one of the roots of our carnival tradition, was that it served as a gathering place for all types of itinerant entertainers, those performing vagabonds of an earlier age—clowns, tightrope walkers, acrobats, contortionists, equestrians, monstrosities, fortune-tellers, puppeteers, and myriad others. As the market and business side of the English fair diminished in the latter part of the eighteenth century, the entertainments and more pleasurable attractions became specialized as menageries, exhibitions, booth theatres, cabinets of curiosity, waxworks, and the like provided components of what would become the modern circus.

The evolution of the circus as we know it, however, is most closely aligned with the equestrian training circle of the eighteenth century. Among the first of these equestrians to demonstrate their skills in England was one Thomas Johnson, who was billed to perform his "wonderful exploits of horsemanship on Durdham Downs." He claimed to be the first person in England to "ride two horses, as fast as they can go, all around the course with one foot on the top of each saddle." Certainly by the middle of the eighteenth century, English riding masters were frequently offering exhibitions combining skills of horsemanship with other acrobatic skills. Although a number of these equestrians might be given credit for being the father of the modern circus, it is Philip Astley (1742–1814) who emerges as the most obvious progenitor. Between 1768 and 1773, Astley, a retired Dragoon sergeant, evolved his "riding school" near the Westminster Bridge at Lambeth into what amounted to a one-ring circus featuring horsemanship acts and ultimately developing not only into the modern circus, but also into a form of theatre called "hippodrama" or "equestrian drama." Astley's efforts prospered, leading to the construction of a number of circus amphitheatres.

European circuses stayed close to Astley's original form, often in fixed locations and permanent circus buildings, but adding in time clowns, acrobats, jugglers, trapeze artists, trained animals, and other common circus acts. As noted earlier, in contrast, the American circus's early trend was toward size and movement, thus setting its ultimate development apart from the Astley tradition and creating a history quite unique in circus annals.

In essence, the early American circus was virtually transported from England, although elements of the circus were already present in the form of itinerant entertainment and the exhibition of animals, the menagerie, some years prior to the establishment of a "circus" proper. Although it is difficult to document the earliest entertainers, we know that a troupe of rope dancers was performing in Philadelphia in 1724; that a performer was juggling and balancing on the slack wire and the tightrope in New York in 1753; that tumblers and rope dancers were in Boston in 1792; and that in the English tradition trick riding might have been seen as early as 1770. A Mr. Faulks was definitely performing feats of horsemanship in Philadelphia in 1771. The exhibition of animals was an even earlier tradition; the menagerie might well be considered the first phase of the modern American circus to be exploited. As early as 1716 the first lion arrived in Boston, followed five years later by the appearance of a camel. A polar bear was exhibited for the first time in Boston in 1733; an orangutan and a tiger arrived together in New York in 1789. Although shows and exhibitions of all varieties were formally forbidden by an act of Congress in 1774, it is not surprising that one of the first circus amusements to be offered after the war was a large menagerie of birds, reptiles, and quadrupeds. It is also worthy of note that whereas the frivolous pleasures offered by such institutions as theatres and circuses were roundly discouraged in early colonial New England, the traveling menagerie was tolerated as an educational venture, as were early museums offering other forms of entertainment in addition to museum artifacts, including live performers and human curiosities. The ultimate evolution of the circus throughout this young country, however, had to wait until the repeal of the ban after the Revolutionary War in 1780.

Although there are numerous records of individual performers presenting circus acts on these shores, including the first native equestrian, Thomas Poole, who appeared first in 1785, it remained for a Scotsman, John Bill Ricketts, to bring the previously disparate elements together. Ricketts arrived in 1792, and, after having first established a riding academy at 12th and Market streets in Philadelphia, he built his own amphitheatre on the general plan of Astley's and in 1793 presented trick riding, a tightrope walker, and a clown.

Ricketts had been a pupil of Charles Hughes, whose Royal Circus at Blackfriar's Bridge in London had been rival to Astley's since 1782. Although there is no documented evidence, Hughes claimed to have visited America in 1770. He did give the modern circus its name, borrowing the Latin word used to describe the chariot courses of Rome, a tradition drastically different from that of the modern circus, although its name association with ancient times has misled some circus historians to trace individual acts to antiquity and to connect the modern circus to Rome's Circus Maximus or even worse, the Flavian Amphitheatre (Colosseum). In truth, there is no requirement that a circus must be presented in a ring. Even though the circle and size of the circus ring were practical and useful for equestrian exhibitions of skill, the shape evolved in modern times. Today there are circuses still using the traditional ring even though they are completely devoid of equestrian acts.

Ricketts, whose circus was even seen by George Washington, was the first to take an American circus on the road, traveling by boat or horseback to appear in the larger cities along the eastern seaboard. Between 1792 and 1799 his circus presented performances in New York, Boston, and Albany, among other cities in the United States and Canada. Frequently Ricketts would erect wooden arenas for their engagements which might last for several months. In 1799 his Philadelphia amphitheatre burned to the ground. Ricketts set sail for England but perished when his ship sank in a violent storm.

The American circus, then, beginning with single acts, slowly evolved into an amalgamation of elements, and attempts to take the circus to the people continued. In 1814, Pepin and Breschard became the first to cross the Allegheny Mountains and offer circus entertainment in the outposts of Pittsburgh, Cincinnati, and elsewhere. Although a number of additional European showmen helped to establish the circus in America, by the late 1820s most of the dozen or so circus troupes were native operations. In 1825 the opening of the Erie Canal made it possible for the growing number of circuses to travel with greater ease into new territory, and the introduction of the circus tent around 1824 or 1825 (recent research suggests that the first tent circus might have been that of J. Purdy Brown in Wilmington, Delaware, in 1825 or 1826) provided an easy way to make more portable a performance enclosure. Among the earlier pioneer circuses under canvas, though not the first, was that of Nathan Howes and Aaron Turner who took to the road in 1827. In 1828 Buckley and Weeks advertised an aggregation of eight wagons, thirty-five horses, and a canvas tent seventy-five feet in diameter and accommodating 800 patrons. With the country's transportation system improving and the population growing, the circus was beginning to expand and, indeed, to prosper.

Parallel with the growing number of circuses was the expansion of the traveling animal menageries. As early as 1796 the animal most clearly associated with the American circus, the elephant, first was exhibited by a Mr. Owen.

The second and the most famous early elephant in the new country, "Old Bet," was purchased at a London auction for $20 and brought to America where Hachaliah Bailey, a New York tavern keeper, bought her, between 1805 and 1810, for $1,000 and exhibited her with great success until 1816.* Bailey was so fond of his "ponderous Pachyderm" that he built the Elephant Hotel in 1825 in his hometown of Somers, New York, erecting before its entrance a monument to "Old Bet" in 1827. Most early American circus pioneers lived in the Somers area, where animals were bred and trained, acts were rehearsed, and tents and wagons were constructed. Somers's prominence in the history of the circus earned it the name "Cradle of the American Circus." It remained the center of the American circus until 1927, when the Ringlings moved their winter quarters in Bridgeport, Connecticut, to Sarasota, Florida.

Bailey's success with "Old Bet" encouraged him to add more animals. Soon other showmen from the Putnam and Westchester County areas followed his example and more traveling menageries were created. In the 1830s menageries were enormous, and expeditions were mounted to bring more exotic animals from Africa. By the end of the first quarter of the nineteenth century, efforts were made to merge the menagerie and the circus, and by the end of the first half of the century the distinctive characteristics of the American circus began to emerge. The circus grew from an equestrian show to the opulent spectacle so characteristic

*A recent survey of elephants in American circuses before 1840 by Stuart Thayer can be found in *Bandwagon* 31 (January–February 1987).

of our circus, although for many years the horse remained the top performer of the animals in the circus menagerie, providing also the means for moving the show from one location to another, especially in rural America. Beginning in the 1830s (some historians say 1837, when a short-lived circus marched through the streets of Albany), the horse made possible one of the American circus's most unique features, the circus parade. The circus and its horse-drawn wagons usually traveled by night, pausing on the outskirts of the next show stop in order to make a triumphal entry for the early morning citizens. In 1846 the Van Amburgh show introduced a highly carved, ornamental chariot to carry its band in parades; others quickly copied this practice. While a magnificent band wagon led the procession, a calliope (pronounced in the circus cally-ope) or steam fiddle (invented in 1856), the most popular of circus musical instruments, provided a loud and raucous conclusion to the spectacle. Although the parade is no more, a large number of the wagons survive in numerous collections, most notably the Circus World Museum in Baraboo, Wisconsin. In 1985 the tradition was revived with a gigantic circus parade through the streets of Milwaukee.

By the early nineteenth century, land as far west as Illinois had been incorporated into the union. Furthermore, from 1800 to 1860 the majority of the population in the burgeoning nation were country dwellers, with major population areas separated by considerable distances. Thus, the nomadic nature of the American circus evolved out of necessity. With poor or nonexistent roads or trails available, other means of transportation were obligatory; thus enterprising showmen turned to water travel via the Ohio and Mississippi rivers. Just as flour, textiles, lantern oil, and other goods, largely inaccessible by land, were delivered to many settlements by water, so inevitably was entertainment, beginning as early as 1831 in the form of floating theatres. The first recorded boat circus (under Gilbert Spalding and Charles Rogers), an early example of the showboat, appeared in 1852. Dan Rice (1823–1900), the most famous of the early American circus clowns, operated his own show for many years along the rivers of America. As circuses explored new means of transportation, competition among circuses became more and more intense. To counter competition, for instance, a merger of several animal companies in the Somers area created in 1835 the first circus trust, which was to become the Zoological Institute.

With growth and competition also came innovation and a long list of circus firsts, many connected to travel and the transportation of the circus. Although many circuses continued to travel over land during the nineteenth century and many wagon shows persevered into this century, the trend was toward greater use of the railroad, allowing for longer trips to major cities and greater profits. In 1838 the circus first used rail travel as transportation (from Forsythe to Macon, Georgia). Although Den Stone was an early pioneer on the rails in 1854, true rail mobility dates from the standardization of railroad gauge in the 1860s. For example, in 1869 Dan Castello's Circus and Menagerie was the first to take a circus across the United States by railroad, just two months after the driving of the golden spike at Promontory Point, Utah. By 1885 fifty or more circuses were on the road; the 1890s and early years of this century witnessed many small railroad circuses traveling across the country. For the most part, motorized transportation and the railroad had totally displaced mule and horse power by the early years of the twentieth century. The circus of Tom Mix is credited with having made the first motorized transcontinental tour of the United States in 1936.

Another important first of the 1840s, a new kind of circus poster, is credited to Richard Sands, who developed his own circus in 1842 and took the first American circus to England in 1843. Sands is believed to have been the first to develop a poster printed in color from wood blocks on rag paper and intended for reuse. The earliest such surviving poster, in the Hertzberg Circus Collection, San Antonio, Texas, measuring approximately ten feet high by nearly five feet wide, advertises the R. Sands & Co. Hippoferaean Arena of 1849.

Travel in the United States was expanded considerably with the establishment of the Morman Trail, coinciding with the migration of the Mormons to Utah beginning in 1847, and the California Trail, expediting travel from Salt Lake City to San Francisco. The 1849 gold rush encouraged the circus and other entertainment forms to move almost immediately west, with the establishment by Joseph Andrew Rowe of the Olympic Circus in San Francisco in 1849.

Following a relatively brief pause necessitated by the Civil War, the American circus continued its growth spurt. With mounting competition, new avenues to attract and excite the public's interest were sought and found with the expansion of the street parade and, one of the American circus's major features, the introduction of multiple rings. Around 1873 Andrew Haight's Great Eastern Circus and Menagerie declared that it would present its show in two rings. At about the same time, William Cameron Coup (1836–95) added a second ring to the circus utilizing the name of P. T. Barnum (1810–91), the famous showman and museum entrepreneur; and in 1881 James A. Bailey (1847–1906) negotiated the merger of several great circus operations, including the Barnum circus, and opened with a three-ring show. By 1885, in fact, when Barnum was briefly merged with the great circus pioneer Adam Forepaugh (d. 1890), their circus had four rings plus two stages placed between them for acrobats. By the 1890s virtually all American circuses had settled on the three-ring format, a trend that in recent years has slowly been reversed. In the nineteenth century, however, and well into our own time, the credo of the American circus was to give the spectator more than he could possibly see at one time, on the basis that bigger is somehow better.

By the latter part of the nineteenth century the circus had completed its amalgamation of the menagerie, the band concert, the sideshow (a term for any auxiliary show), and the street parade; the key ingredients of the American circus were in place. The period between 1830 and 1870 saw hundreds of American circuses come into existence, ranging from impressive and well-equipped railroad shows to miniscule family circuses that were limited to miserable country back roads. Many of the most prominent in the history of the American circus, each with a wonderful history too extensive for this brief introduction, date from this era, including such stalwarts as the various shows utilizing the name of the "Lion King" (Isaac Van Amburgh), the George F. Bailey Circus, the several circuses of Seth B. Howes, the Mabie Brothers Circus, the Yankee (Fayette Ludovic) Robinson Circus, the John Robinson Circus (a name attached to circuses longer than any other), the Spalding and Rogers Circus, the Dan Castello Circus,

15

the Dan Rice Circus, and the W. W. Cole Circus.

A major turning point of the American circus dates from around 1871, the beginning of what has been called the golden age of the American circus, reaching its apogee about 1917. The two decades of the 1870s and 1880s are most remarkable for the major mergers that occurred, creating enormous circus operations that ultimately swallowed up many smaller operations, not however until the circus reached its peak period in 1903 with approximately ninety-eight circuses and menageries in existence. The circuitous path some of the most important mergers took also helps to account for the most confusing period in circus annals.

An early merger dates from around 1870 when Seth B. Howes purchased the American rights to the title "Great London" from the British showman "Lord" George Sanger, passing the rights on to his nephews. The 1873 financial panic helped cause the Howes' show to flounder; eventually, James E. Cooper (1832–92) and James A. Bailey, who had merged their operations in 1873, acquired this circus, creating in 1879 Howes' Great London and Sanger's Royal British Menagerie. In 1871 William Cameron Coup and Dan Castello persuaded the showman P. T. Barnum, following the destruction by fire for the second time of his famous American Museum, to become a partner in a circus enterprise. The circus utilizing the famous Barnum name opened on April 10, 1871, in Brooklyn with the largest tent and the greatest number of men and horses in the history of the circus. Using his unique talent for promotion and overstatement, Barnum billed the 1873 version of the show "P. T. Barnum's Great Traveling World's Fair Consisting of Museum, Menagerie, Caravan, Hippodrome,

Gallery of Statuary and Fine Arts, Polytechnic Institute, Zoological Garden and 100,000 Curiosities, combined with Dan Castello's, Sig. Sebastian's and Mr. D'Atelie's Grand Triple Equestrian and Hippodramatic Exposition." A true circus mouthful if there ever was one!

In 1874, due to ill health and to Barnum's tendency to loan his name to other shows in addition to Coup's, a split developed and Coup finally sold his interest to Barnum. In 1876 the title of the circus first appeared as "P. T. Barnum's New and Greatest Show on Earth," even though Barnum had minimal involvement with the operation, depending on his numerous assistant managers to run the show. In 1880 Barnum joined with James A. Bailey, who bought out his partner Cooper in 1881, and James L. Hutchinson to form "P. T. Barnum's Greatest Show on Earth, Howes' Great London Circus and Sanger's Royal British Menagerie." This lucrative partnership survived until 1885 when Barnum refused to deal further with Bailey. Bailey sold his interest and retired. Barnum and Hutchinson, in turn, sold portions of their interest to James Cooper and William Washington Cole so that four entrepreneurs now controlled the show. In 1887, after Barnum had experienced a number of setbacks, including the loss of a Madison Square Garden contract to the rival Adam Forepaugh Circus, Bailey was persuaded to return, rejoin the partnership, and, ultimately, to acquire a 50 percent interest by buying out Cooper and Cole. Bailey, in full control, added his name to the now familiar "Barnum & Bailey Greatest Show on Earth." Today's corporate mergers and takeovers have nothing on these procedures! The story of this most important merger, however, actually did not end there. Bailey, in time, came to terms with Forepaugh by dividing territory and after Barnum's death bought the complete circus holdings of the Barnum estate, thus becoming something of a circus czar, at least for a brief time, for five brothers from the Middle West would soon successfully challenge Bailey's complete control.

In the meantime, the golden age saw the continuance of a number of the older circuses, competing or operating in their own regional circuits, plus the emergence of newer, prominent circuses including the Sells Brothers Circus, the Great Wallace Circus, and the Lemen Brothers Circus. Of all these newer circus names, only Ringling has sustained its overwhelming prominence, even though these brothers (Al, Otto, Alf T., Charles, and John) from Baraboo, Wisconsin, were Johnny-Come-Latelies on the circus scene with no involvement in show business until 1882. After viewing a traveling circus in their hometown, they began to stage their own variety show around Wisconsin, followed in 1884 by their first true circus under the guidance of the elder showman Yankee Robinson, whose name was joined to theirs in the show's title. By 1890 their success had put their show on the rails; two years later they were traveling through a dozen states with thirty-one railroad cars, and in 1895, after adding more circus acts and animals to their menageries, they ventured outside of the Midwest and entered Barnum & Bailey's territory in New England. Strategies reminiscent of the mergers noted earlier followed, climaxing in 1907, the year after Bailey's death, with the purchase by the Ringlings of the Bailey circus properties. Finally, in 1919 the Ringling Brothers merged the two circuses, and on March 29, 1919, at Madison Square Garden, the gigantic "Ringling Brothers and Barnum & Bailey Combined Shows," dubbed the "big one," began its history. Various competitors tried to curtail the Ringling's power, but the circus had become big business and their efforts were fruitless.

By 1910 the circus's decline from its halcyon days was already beginning, gaining momentum as the Ringling operation edged out competition. In 1905 Barnum & Bailey eliminated their free parade, a victim of an unsustainable cost escalation that had begun to steal their profits. Even the Ringling's circus, with the task of moving its tented city on 100 railroad cars with 1,500 performers and employees and an enormous menagerie, discontinued their parade at the end of the 1920 season. In truth, circus parades, epitomizing to the public the gigantic scale of the circus, were often such good shows themselves that patrons, satisfied by the preshow hoopla, stayed away from the big top. In an attempt to be bigger and bigger and more and more spectacular, enormous sums were spent on specially designed wagons. The "Two Hemisphere" wagon, for example, cost Barnum & Bailey in 1896 $40,000 and required a team of forty horses to pull the bulky vehicle. The elimination of the menagerie was not far behind the demise of the parade, and, although there are perhaps two dozen tent shows still in existence, even the big top would practically disappear, symbolically dealt its death blow when Ringling Brothers and Barnum & Bailey ceased performances under canvas in 1956, the end result of management and labor difficulties.

Meanwhile, though large competing circuses would vanish from the scene, improved highways and motorized vehicles helped create a number of smaller tent shows that began moving by truck in the 1920s and 1930s. Of the seven circuses photographed for this book, two (Kelly-Miller and Beatty-Cole) date from this period. More setbacks occurred during the 1940s and 1950s when the larger circuses—the Clyde Beatty, the King Brothers, and the Ringling shows—experienced a series of disasters and crises. Still, the Ringling operation was saved from potential oblivion in 1967 when Irvin Feld, often referred to as the modern-day P. T. Barnum, and his brother Izzy purchased it from the Ringling brothers' descendents in 1967 for $8 million. In a typically Barnumesque gesture, Feld sealed the deal in the ruins of Rome's Colosseum. Moving the circus into efficient but antiseptic indoor arenas, the Felds were able to sell the circus to Mattel Inc. (the toy company) in 1971 for an estimated $50 million in stock, Feld being retained as its president, producer, and chief executive officer. In 1982 when Feld and his son, now running the show, bought the circus back for $22.8 million, Feld commented that "the good Lord never meant for a circus to be owned by a corporation." Feld, who died in 1984, has been succeeded by his son, Kenneth.

The Decline of the Circus

Although the Felds have been amazingly successful in selling their circus, convincing the patron that the circus is bigger and better than ever, with two large units on the road each season playing most major American cities, the truth is quite the contrary. David Hammarstrom in *Behind the Big Top* (1980) describes the current Ringling Brothers show as "a big splash of color with less heads, more feathers, and a strong solo star around which to build each show." Indeed, a "city that traveled by night" carried several thousand individuals in the 1920s; today a large traveling circus might employ a couple of hundred, and even this number is rare.

Most circuses today lead tenuous existences and are, in fact, faint shadows of what once was. Perhaps the reasons for the decline are obvious, although speculations and causes continue to be proposed. In the course of this essay a number have been mentioned, but to these might be added the rising cost of gasoline, especially in the 1960s and 1970s, the cost of animal food, an increase in performers' salaries (long extremely low), tent expenses (prices have more than tripled in recent years), the disasters that have plagued the circus (in particular the Hartford fire of 1944, killing 185 persons and leading to lawsuits totaling about 4 million dollars), the attempts to overglamourize the circus, and the emergence of television as a competitive media. Each of these may have been a contributing factor, although as Marcello Truzzi has persuasively illustrated in *Sociology and Everyday Life* (1968), it would be a mistake to attribute too much to any one, and indeed arguments can be made to dismiss several. For example, although television may have been a factor in the circus's decline, this decline was well under way before national television. Today, ironically, even with cable, there has developed a sense of boredom with canned and edited entertainment, and audiences seem to thirst again for live, spontaneous performance. The circus, with its sense of danger and even the possibility of death, might profit from this turnaround. Certainly it is fascinating to watch the revival of interest in professional wrestling, for example, after a very slack period of interest of almost a quarter of a century.

Truzzi, I believe, correctly identifies the major reasons for the initial decline when he says the changes began when the circus altered or eliminated its unique elements. Indeed, I contend that most unique American entertainment forms experienced their demises in much the same way; at least the circus, unlike all other forms originating in the same time frame, still persists. Specifically Truzzi notes three themes that have undergone drastic change: (1) the romantic mystique of the traveling community, symbolized by the giant Big Top and the circus train, now all but gone from the scene; (2) the panoramic spectacle, symbolized by the circus parade, a thing of the past; and (3) the exotic and mysterious, symbolized by the wild animals and the sideshow freaks. Even the most exotic animal is recognized by most of us these days, with zoos commonplace and televised nature programs taking us to the remotest areas of the world. Medical science has taken care of most human oddities, and in our more polite society we frown at those who stare at those with physical deformities. Indeed, exhibition of human freaks is now illegal in many states. The few sideshows left now exhibit primarily man-made attractions such as sword-swallowers, fire-eaters, and tatooed men or women. Ultimately, the true reason for the circus's decline in recent years is simply that man's natural passion for mystery and awe has succumbed to the age of technology, the wonders of the modern media (it is hard to top or even equal a *Star Wars*), and a sophistication that verges on the cynical and blasé (even rural America can no longer claim innocence and naiveté). The modern traveling circus is now faced with new problems, making survival ever more difficult, including the rising cost (or even inaccessibility) of liability insurance (Clyde Beatty–Cole Brothers currently pays $1,700 per day; Franzen Brothers reported that in 1986 their liability insurance had risen 1100% in a year), which has also frightened away potential sponsors, the lifeblood of many small circuses; antiphone promotion sentiment in many areas, a result of a few unscrupulous operators; and the harassment of circuses by animals rights groups, though circuses have been found innocent of charges brought against them by the Society for the Prevention of Cruelty to Animals.

Any way one tries to interpret current circus statistics or the causes for decline, a circus renaissance is not on the horizon, although circuses are likely to endure for years as long as they touch something central in its audience, something without an age barrier. Robert Toll, in *On with the Show* (1976), and others have suggested that one of the appeals of the circus is its closeness to nature beneath its showy facade and its ability to transcend natural laws. Perhaps Toll is correct when he says that the circus is largely a relic, "a nostalgic re-creation of the nature-based rituals of an earlier day." Still, as of 1986, the circus is not a totally endangered species, and a few showmen with affinities to earlier traditions continue to try to return the circus to some of the ways it used to be.

Earl Chapin May recorded in *The Circus From Rome to Ringling* (1932) that during the 1870s some forty-odd shows trouped through the South. By 1893 a dozen of those moved by rail, competing for top territory, and less than twenty years later the number had tripled. As noted earlier, 1903 was the peak year: three dozen shows traveled on a combined total of 675 railroad cars; an equal number of smaller circuses used highways and back roads. By the Depression the number dwindled drastically; after the 1938 season only thirty or so struggled to survive. By 1956 there were only a couple of dozen tenters, most touring by truck. This number, however, has remained fairly constant up to the present. According to *The Bandwagon*, the journal of the Circus Historical Society, during the 1985 season, roughly mid-March to late October for most tented circuses, there were at least eighty-five shows that called themselves circuses, although only the usual two dozen really came close to the real thing. Other than Ringling Brothers, the major circuses (and tent shows) were Clyde Beatty–Cole Brothers, Circus Vargas (although this noble show seemed to be in trouble), Carson & Barnes, "the biggest thing that moved every night," and the Kelly-Miller Circus. That season two shows from the previous year did not reopen, but four more tent efforts debuted. A large number of contemporary circuses are those that play for Shrine charities, although about half of the total are very small shows playing fairs, ball parks, outdoor arenas, shopping malls, gyms, or similar existing spaces, frequently on an ad hoc basis, not with the community atmosphere and cooperative living of the traveling tent show. Still, as *Bandwagon* concludes, unlike the some 280 carnivals that tour the country, the American circus today still has a kind of purity about it; it is still what we thought it was when we were kids. Many performers continue to come from old circus families; many are serious artists perfecting their skills, skills and artistry that are certainly more wonderful to watch and to empathize with in their live, imperfect form than in edited versions on television.

Edwin Martin has preserved for us images of some of these remaining circuses, possibly the final vestiges of the last chapter of the American circus's evolution. The last fifty years of the annals of the American circus are represented here with scenes on lots of seven circuses with founding dates ranging from 1935 (Clyde Beatty–Cole Brothers) to the Toby Tyler Circus (1984); Kelly-Miller was established in 1938; Hoxie Brothers, which served as the source for Fred Powledge's *Mud Show: A Circus Season* (1975), dates from 1948–49, though it is now defunct; Carson & Barnes began in 1969 (there was never a Carson or a Barnes, by the way), Franzen Brothers in 1974, and the Roberts Brothers the same year, though the present show of that name is three years old.

As stated earlier, my intention is not to explain these photographs. A few comparative comments, however, might be appropriate. The Clyde Beatty–Cole Brothers Circus, out of De Land, Florida, is the largest tent show represented in Martin's collection, and one of the most successful. This three-ring show travels over 9,000 miles annually and plays approximately 115 cities, primarily through the mid-Atlantic states and New England, over an eight-month period. It boasts the largest big top in use, though this is probably not completely true, constructed of 8,200 yards of canvas (a new tent costing $165,000 was assembled first in May 1986). Carson & Barnes, one of the larger traveling circuses with five rings, and Al G. Kelly–Miller Brothers both winter in Hugo, Oklahoma, at one time the home to five or six tent circuses. Carson & Barnes travels almost twice the distance of Beatty-Cole through twenty states to find its audience. When they took to the road in March 1986, they numbered among them 80 brightly painted vehicles, 250 people, a hippo, a rhino, a giraffe, assorted lions, tigers, llamas, horses, donkeys, zebras, fifteen elephants, and goats. Kelly-Miller is a three-ring small-town circus with about eighteen displays that moves on four or five semis plus about fifteen to twenty-five mobile homes and campers and plays under a 90-by-

190-foot Scola Teloni vinyl big top accommodating about 1,500. This organization, including about sixty-five people, plays eight months over a 12,000-mile route including seventeen states and several Canadian provinces. Franzen Brothers, Roberts Brothers, and Toby Tyler are typical of the somewhat smaller tent shows still struggling for survival. Franzen, which winters in Florida, travels up the Atlantic seaboard and in the Midwest and finishes with a southern swing. The owner, Wayne Franzen, a former high-school industrial arts teacher, is virtually a one-man circus, presenting the cat act, a camel and llama act, a twelve-pony drill, and Okha the elephant in his green 120-by-80-foot tent housing a single large ring. Billed as "America's Favorite Show," this circus offers acts that some circus critics believe surpass the quality of competing tent shows. Both Toby Tyler and Roberts are three-ring circuses, the former spotlighting in 1986 a large, new Italian top of red and gold stripes and boasting a sizable midway, including a side show top and a menagerie exhibit featuring two hippos, two ostriches, forty horses, twelve elephants, nine tigers, two lions, two camels, two guanacos, and two zebras.

The Appeal of the Circus

So what has been so special about the American circus for more than two centuries? Why has it attracted and fascinated people of all ages and backgrounds for so long—and for many still does? Despite all that has been written about the demise of the American circus, why has this form of live popular entertainment managed to defy competition from radio, television, and motion pictures when other forms have become nothing more than a nostalgic memory—or, like the dime museum, been forgotten altogether? And how has the circus in its various forms affected the cultural development of our country?

Throughout this introduction speculations as to some of the answers to these questions have been posed. Others might be tossed into the mixer; each individual fan of the circus no doubt has other very personal and perhaps unexplainable reasons as well.

For Mark Twain's Huckleberry Finn, the circus was simply "the splendidist sight that ever was." The late William Lyon Phelps, a noted professor of English at Yale University, once commented that "Heaven lay about me in my infancy, and it took a circular shape. From the moment I entered the great tent until I emerged some hours later I was in Paradise." Phelps went on to say that even after he was over sixty he still loved the circus. He continued to attend the circus, not to see if he could "recapture" his childish enthusiasm; "I go because I want to go, because the circus ring draws me, and it ought to, with contripetal force." Indeed, Phelps and others have noted that if you have imagination the delight of the circus does not lessen much with age but seems to change little year after year.

Granted, as Jill Freedman observes in her collection of circus photographs, *Circus Days*, the circus certainly can be an "exuberant place, like childhood; a celebration of the joy of just being alive." William Saroyan expressed the appeal in *My Name Is Aram* when he wrote: "The circus was everything, everything else we knew wasn't. It was adventure, travel, danger, skill, grace, romance, comedy, peanuts, popcorn, chewing-gum and soda-water." For me, it was also the special circus smells and sounds. Certainly if we lose the circus one more piece of life's magic will disappear with it. However, if the circus's principal appeal is a recapturing of the fun and romance of youth, a way to cling to something permanent and enduring, such a nostalgic link could just as well point toward the final deathblow, for it could be argued that the nostalgia many feel for circuses proves that the true circus is almost gone.

The circus can also be seen as a kind of microcosm of life. Thomas W. Duncan, writing in the *Saturday Review* in April 1954, suggested that within the oval of the hippodrome track "the arena of life is epitomized"—that is, the externals of life are exposed by the "crude dangers, the lofty ventures, man's mastery of the lower animals, man's acrobatic victories." No hint of man's inner nature seems to exist until the clowns enter. "They are gently and obliquely suggesting that this brawny, bespangled, victorious, stentorian fellow called man has also . . . a soul. If he has his triumphs, he has his defeats as well." As a historian, I believe also that since the circus has reflected changes occurring in American society as a whole during the years of its evolution, it can serve as a source for shedding some light on these changes and can contribute to a better understanding of ourselves and of the society in which we now live.

For my money, the circus can be wonderful theatre, with all the suspense, character, and plotting of a good mystery on stage. Certainly it has the spectacle, the color, and the showmanship of the best of entertainment. And, with very few exceptions, the better performers are true artists, working constantly to perfect not only their skills but their artistry. If taken seriously, then, each time one goes to a circus there should be a new sense of pleasant discovery, even in the repetition of a performance, an aesthetic pleasure not dissimilar to looking many times at a great painting or reading again a wonderful piece of literature. There is an intangible quality about the circus that is difficult to explain.

Of all the myriad reasons given for the circus's survival and appeal, the most frequently discussed, and the most controversial, is the notion that all circus acts, in one way or another, are demonstrations of mortality. An assistant manager of Ringling Brothers was recently quoted in my local paper as having decried this notion: "I don't think the mentality of the patron is to see a death-defying act as much as the skill involved. When they go to the Olympics, they don't go hoping someone will get hurt. They want to see things they can't do." True enough, but there is a difference between the attraction a contest holds for most of us and the observation of a well-packaged skill, with all the trappings to enhance the sense of danger involved. The circus may no longer triumph over spectacle or the bizarre; we have seen Oz (and been there) too many times. As obsolete and commonplace as these elements may now be, the circus as microcosm or metaphor for life, still a triumph over conditions, continues to attract us. It can even be suggested that many circus acts enhance the idea of life's mortality with their very names, such as "Slide-for-Life" and the "Death Ride"—the former a tightrope artist gliding *down* an inclined wire; the latter a motorcyclist gunning his way *up* an inclined wire.

One author has posed the notion that the trapeze artists, sailing through the air, are defying not death so much as life; "it is easier to die in such an act than it is to live." It may be a morbid suggestion that spectators come to the circus to see how close a performer comes to death, and the closer they come the better the act. It would also be naive to ignore, for example, that the public over the years flocked to see the "Great Wallendas" defy death, when death and injury in their family on the high wire was a well-publicized reality, climaxing with the ten-story fall and death of Karl Wallenda in 1978. The act, however, goes on. There is no question that the circus artists challenge us with the apparent danger of many of their acts and that they become to some extent our scapegoats, risking death so that we don't have to, giving us a kind of existential thrill from them. Even the foolish antics of the clowns exaggerate and mock our vices and virtues.

Undeniably, circus artists are constantly attempting to top themselves, for accomplishments of the past become stale and even boring to the audience, even though the danger may not have lessened. When Miguel Angel Vazquez publicly became the first circus flyer to achieve the quadruple somersault on July 10, 1982, it was like the breaking of the four-minute mile. This accomplishment had eluded generations of performers; now that several flyers have surpassed the triple, including in 1985 Ruben Caballero (the first time under canvas), the trapeze act can be exploited anew. Now the goal is the quad and a half and even, perhaps fifteen years away, the quintuple somersault. If death-defying acts, then, are not one of the circus's major appeals, the element of danger is undeniably always present, as much for the worker on the floor or the sawdust as for the trapeze artists near the roof or the top of the tent. Safety precautions are certainly taken but there are no guarantees.

Visual Representation of the Circus

There is an old and honored tradition of showing the circus visually. On the one hand much of this must be classified as kitsch or, in the case of photographic documentation, photojournalism with a minimum of aesthetic quality or even the representation of good photography. Martin's photographs clearly belong in the category of aesthetic objects and excellent photography, not only important circus documents but artistic representations of intrinsic value.

Visual artists for centuries have been entranced by the circus, drawn, as Alan Ray, supervisor of museum operations at the New York State Museum in Albany, has suggested to its "chameleon-like qualities, the tension between fantasy and suffering exhibited through the clown or the freak. They have seen their own exertions mirrored in the superhuman achievement of the trapeze artist or tightrope walker, and they have compared their own destinies with the popular caprice directed towards performers. . . ." A catalogue of the great artists through history fascinated by the circus would include Picasso, Fernand Leger, Alexander Calder, Toulouse-Lautrec, Seurat, Tissot, Daumier, Renoir, Georges Roualt, Walt Kuhn, Matisse, Chagall, Hopper, Hogarth, Charles Hammond, W. H. Brown, Reginald Marsh, Chaim Gross, Robert Motherwell, Jules Pascin, Max Beckman, John Steuart Curry, and no doubt many others.

As we have attempted to demonstrate, the myriad reasons for the circus's appeal no doubt apply to artists as well as spectators. Indeed, one can see in the circus living caricatures of all the people found in our larger society. The variety of subjects and moods is enormous, the symbolism striking. Dean Jensen, an art critic for the *Milwaukee Sentinal* and a circus expert (author of *The Biggest, The Smallest, The Longest, The Shortest,* published in 1975), believes the artist can become a part of the circus as an impresario, identifying with the entire show; as a performer, empathizing with its highly individual characters; or as a spectator, studying at ringside, or even on the back lot, the nuances of movement and the relationships of color and light and shadow.

The most common forms of circus art, and the earliest, preceded only by eighteenth-century prints of performers, were the lithographs and posters dating from the mid-nineteenth century. Notable were the lithographs of Currier and Ives and early Mathew Brady photographs of such attractions as General Tom Thumb, Chang and Eng, the original Siamese twins, and Jane Campbell, the fat lady; many wonderful lithographs were used for the covers of circus sheet music, still to be seen in various archives.

It was noted in the historical overview that the circus poster was a significant predecessor of methods now associated with Madison Avenue advertising techniques. Large posters were first seen in the early 1830s; multicolored woodcuts and lithographs appeared about 1850. Incredibly large quantities of posters, small and large ones, were used daily by circuses, with a team of advance men arriving in an area and, within a twenty-mile radius, putting up from 5,000 to 8,000 sheets of "paper," as circus posters and bills were called. (A standard single sheet measured twenty-eight inches by forty-two inches.) For rural areas and larger towns alike, the poster created a great sense of excitement at a time when American life was quite isolated. Although circus promoters rarely intended to deceive the public with the circus poster, there was a clear attempt to express the hugeness of everything about the circus coming to town, thus combining a wondrous mix of excess, naiveté, and technical sophistication. Even these works of fantasy are revelatory, both about the circus of the time and about our society.

The production of circus posters evolved into a true art form. A number of lithography companies specialized in show printing, most notably the Strobridge Lithographing Company in Cincinnati, which did its first circus work about 1867. Their work was of the highest quality. And, although the majority of artists who designed circus graphics remain unknown, several became identified with this kind of design work and a few signed their posters. Notable among these artists have been Charles Livington Bull, Matt Morgan, H. A. Ogden, Emil Rothengaten, Adolphe and Otto Rimanoczy, Verne Meyer, Joseph Hornik, Joe Schermerle, Hap Hadley, E. McKnight Kauffer, Lawson Wood, Bill Bailey, Forrest Freeland, and even the well-known theatrical scenic designer Norman Bel Geddes.

Likewise, a number of famous photographers, from Mathew Brady to Diane Arbus, have been attracted by the circus, and although candid and rather unimaginative photographs exist by the thousands, some, like those of Martin or Jill Freedman, transcend the commonplace. The first notable circus photographs date from around the Civil War, when photographers, in addition to Brady, such as Charles Eisenmann of New York, specialized in carte-de-visite and slightly larger cabinet-size photos of freaks and individual performers. Edward J. Kelty and his Century Studio in New York City produced, annually, twelve-by-twenty-inch group pictures of circus personnel as well as other photographs documenting circus life during the 1920s and 1930s. Also notable during this period were the portraits of August Sander. In the late 1920s clown Pete Mardo snapped circus pictures which he sold to circus fans; similar candid or often posed photographs became commonplace.

Martin's photographs are in many ways unique, for unlike most of the visual images of the circus that exist, from the past or the present, he makes no attempt to fictionalize or romanticize his subject. Instead, his objective has been to make interesting, and, I would add, artistic photographs, depicting all aspects of contemporary life on a mud show, collectively offering a portrait of this way of life and this special slice of American popular entertainment. I know of no comparable portfolio of circus photographs. Freedman's *Circus Days* (1975) is the nearest in concept, though unlike the long-range commitment of Martin, Freedman's project focused on one circus during a two-month period on tour in the Northeast. Martin's, in contrast, show us aspects of seven circuses over several years in all parts of the country and in winter quarters. More important, while Freedman's photographs, avoiding all performance within the big top, either tell a story, amplified by written text, or demonstrate an activity, Martin's in my view cover a wider range of subject and require less explanation. There is also, in my opinion, despite the clear appreciation I have for Freedman's artistry, a more pronounced aesthetic quality to Martin's photographs.

So, with no further ado, here is Edwin Martin's evocation of a dying institution—the American traveling tent circus!

Note on Sources

Although there is no one definitive history of the American circus, there is certainly an extensive literature on the circus, and much of the material for an expansive history

34

is available, appearing, for example, in the circus trade journals: before the turn of the century the *Clipper;* after, the *Billboard.* In addition, important historical articles, written largely by avid circus fans and amateur historians, are contained in *The White Tops* (1927–present), the magazine of the Circus Fans Association of America, founded in 1926, and *Bandwagon* (1957–present), the journal of the Circus Historical Society, founded in 1939. The latter is especially good for essays on individual circuses. The major guide to circus literature is Raymond Toole-Stott's *Circus and Allied Arts, A World Bibliography,* published in four volumes (1958–71) by Harpur in Derby, England. However, for a more focused assessment of material on the American circus, two of my own reference works might prove more immediately useful: *American and English Popular Entertainment* (Gale Research, 1980) and *Variety Entertainment and Outdoor Amusements* (Greenwood Press, 1982). Since the publication of the latter source, a number of new books on the American circus have appeared, most notably the following: Bill Ballantine, *Clown Alley* (Little, Brown, 1982); Wilton Eckley, *The American Circus* (Twayne Publishers, 1984); Charles Philip Fox, *Circus Baggage Stock* (Pruett Publishing, 1983); Charles Philip Fox and Tom Parkinson, *Billers, Banner and Bombast: The Story of Circus Advertising* (Pruett Publishing, 1985); Joanne Carol Joys, *The Wild Animal Trainer in America* (Pruett, 1983); F. Beverly Kelly, *It was Better Than Work* (The Patrice Press, 1982); Copeland MacAllister, *Uncle Gus and the Circus* (self-published, 1984); and Stuart Thayer, *Annals of the American Circus 1830–1847* (Peanut Butter Publishing, 1986). The standard histories of the American circus are still George L. Chindahl's *A History of the Circus in America* (Caxton, 1959), Fox and Parkinson's *The Circus in America* (Country Beautiful, 1969), and Earl Chapin May's *The Circus from Rome to Ringling* (Duffield and Green, 1932). George Speaight's *A History of the Circus* (A. S. Barnes, 1980) devotes a major portion of his book to the American circus, with some documentation.

Photographs

Center pole holes, Lake Isabella, California, 1984 (Carson & Barnes).

Wet lot, Cedar City, Missouri,
1985 (Carson & Barnes).

Tear down, Radcliff, Kentucky,
1985 (Kelly–Miller Brothers).

Koto, Milwaukee, Wisconsin,
1986 (Carson & Barnes).

Three clowns (Koto, Rhonda, Phil), Milwaukee, Wisconsin, 1986 (Carson & Barnes).

EJ at the front door, Window
Rock, Arizona, 1984 (Carson &
Barnes).

Five clowns (Flip, Phil, Mariah, EJ, and Bob), Bullhead City, Arizona, 1984 (Carson & Barnes).

Chained elephant (Libby),
Adams, Wisconsin, 1984
(Carson & Barnes).

Winter quarters (Bones), Hugo,
Oklahoma, 1985 (Carson &
Barnes, winter quarters).

Ostriches, New Brunswick, New
Jersey, 1986 (Toby Tyler).

Trapeze play, Effingham, Illinois, 1985 (Carson & Barnes).

Memorial Day parade (Sandy),
Brick Town, New Jersey, 1986
(Clyde Beatty–Cole Brothers).

Two clowns in the cookhouse
(Phil and Johnny), Richmond,
Indiana, 1986 (Carson &
Barnes).

Guest clowns, Richmond,
Indiana, 1986 (Carson &
Barnes).

Two couples by the backdoor
(Nancy and Lalo, Lolis and
Alejandro), Marshfield,
Wisconsin, 1984 (Carson &
Barnes).

Sideshow pitch (Zippo, Donna,
Harry), Bucyrus, Ohio, 1985
(Kelly–Miller Brothers).

Highwire ascent (Isreal, Ruben),
Litchfield, Illinois, 1985 (Carson
& Barnes).

Elephant and house, De Land,
Florida, 1986 (Clyde Beatty–
Cole Brothers, winter quarters).

Tatooed lady (Dan, Lola,
Louie), Stirling, New Jersey,
1986 (Toby Tyler).

Clown in trailer (Phil), Fairview,
Oklahoma, 1984 (Carson &
Barnes).

Backdoor play (Mariel, Mattie Lou, Phil), New Richmond, Wisconsin, 1984 (Carson & Barnes).

Elephant practice (Red), Hugo,
Oklahoma, 1985 (Carson &
Barnes, winter quarters).

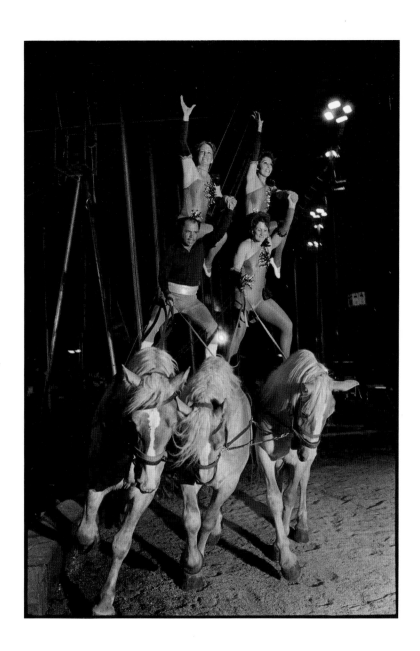

Bareback pyramid (Alfredo,
Lucy, Moira, Chava),
Milwaukee, Wisconsin, 1986
(Carson & Barnes).

Elephant act (Pat), Eau Claire,
Wisconsin, 1984 (Carson &
Barnes).

Dancing elephants (Lucy),
Greensburg, Indiana, 1984
(Carson & Barnes).

Pat and Rex, Milwaukee,
Wisconsin, 1986 (Carson &
Barnes).

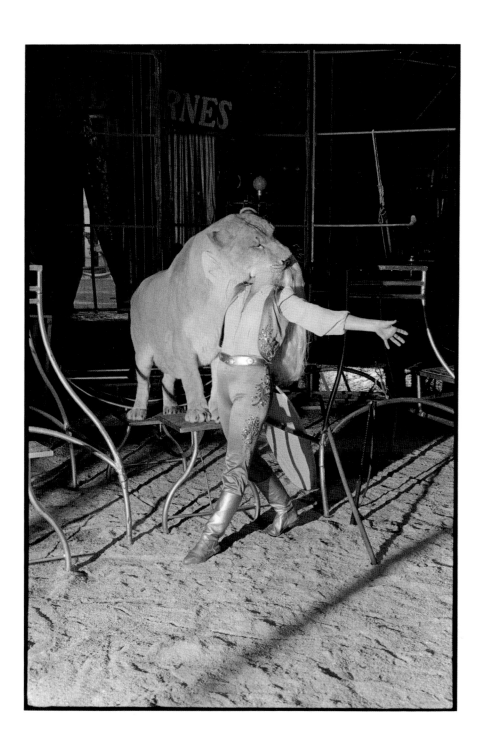

Candy Butcher, Shiprock, New
Mexico, 1984 (Carson &
Barnes).

Rolling globes, Aztec, New Mexico, 1984 (Carson & Barnes).

Two clowns (one asleep; Phil
and EJ), Dalhart, Texas, 1984
(Carson & Barnes).

Winded clown (Bob; EJ, Greg),
Santa Fe, New Mexico, 1984
(Carson & Barnes).

Cookhouse tent (Phil), New
Richmond, Wisconsin, 1984
(Carson & Barnes).

Pedicure (Allan and Becky),
New Richmond, Wisconsin,
1984 (Carson & Barnes).

On the ropes, Elroy, Wisconsin,
1984 (Carson & Barnes).

Libby, Durango, Colorado,
1984 (Carson & Barnes).

Elephants and tent, Nashville, Tennessee, 1983 (Carson & Barnes).

Bareback practice (Loyal
family), Hugo, Oklahoma, 1985
(Carson & Barnes, winter
quarters).

Bareback rider (Lucy),
Milwaukee, Wisconsin, 1986
(Carson & Barnes).

Overture, New Brunswick, New
Jersey, 1986 (Toby Tyler).

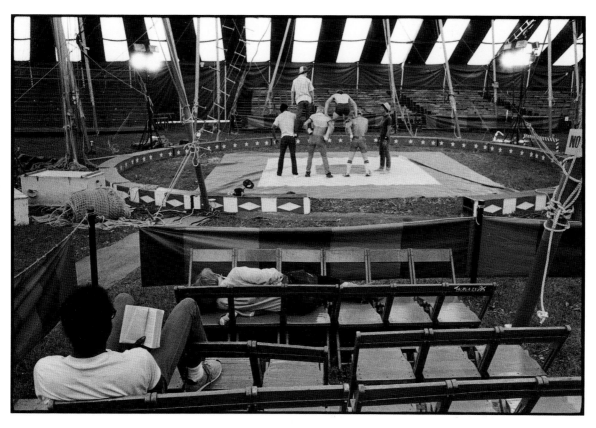

Workingmen's dreams, Willow
Grove, Pennsylvania, 1986
(Clyde Beatty–Cole Brothers).

Lion taming (Pat), Bullhead
City, Arizona, 1984 (Carson &
Barnes).

Kelly, Willow Grove,
Pennsylvania, 1986 (Clyde
Beatty–Cole Brothers).

Setting the flag, Rainelle, West
Virginia, 1986 (Roberts
Brothers).

Mabel leaps (Pat), Cedar City, Missouri, 1985 (Carson & Barnes).

Big lasso (Jay), Bucyrus, Ohio,
1985 (Kelly–Miller Brothers).

Tired camel, Radcliff, Kentucky,
1985 (Kelly–Miller Brothers).

Sleeping clown (EJ), Oshkosh,
Wisconsin, 1984 (Carson &
Barnes).

Watching the setup, Marshfield,
Wisconsin, 1984 (Carson &
Barnes).

Waiting for spec (Pancho et al.),
Greensburg, Indiana, 1984
(Carson & Barnes).

Elephant trio (Chris, Nina, Ron), Radcliff, Kentucky, 1985 (Kelly–Miller Brothers).

Trained giraffe (Lena), Radcliff, Kentucky, 1985 (Kelly–Miller Brothers).

Flying trapeze (Alejandro and
Bruno), Eau Claire, Wisconsin,
1984 (Carson & Barnes).

Tony, Lost Creek, West Virginia,
1986 (Roberts Brothers).

Red reading, Hugo, Oklahoma, 1985 (Carson & Barnes, winter quarters).

Safety net repair (Herminio),
Willow Grove, Pennsylvania,
1986 (Clyde Beatty–Cole
Brothers).

Retired clown (Diamond Jim
Parker), Gibsonton, Florida,
1986.

Pete pushes the cats, Brick
Town, New Jersey, 1986 (Clyde
Beatty–Cole Brothers).

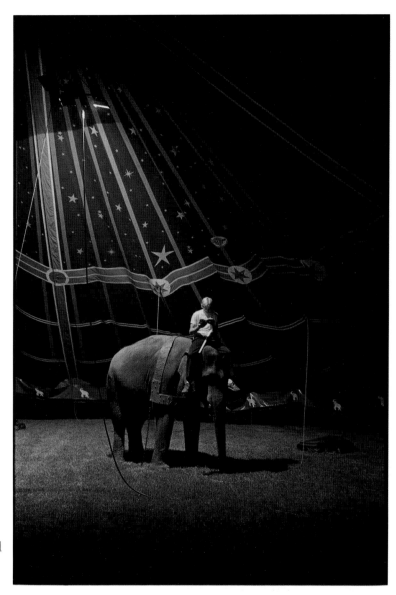

Waiting for tear down (Jim and Nina), St. Marys, Ohio, 1985 (Kelly–Miller Brothers).

Skin and Bones (Mariah and
Bob), Olney, Illinois, 1986
(Carson & Barnes).

Billy, Brick Town, New Jersey, 1986 (Clyde Beatty–Cole Brothers).

Trapeze practice (Maricela),
Martinsville, Indiana, 1984
(Carson & Barnes).

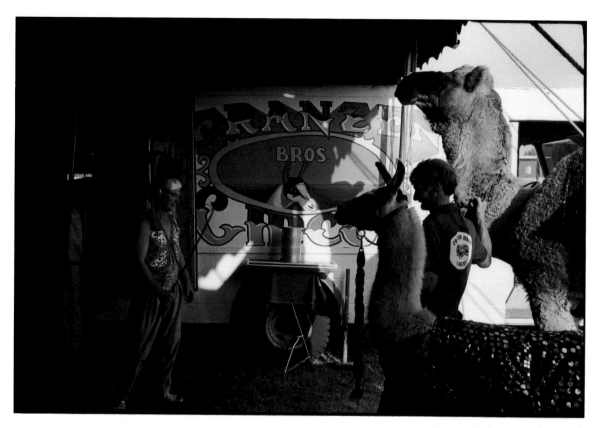

Mixed animal revue (Wayne and
Chuck), Tell City, Indiana, 1985
(Franzen Brothers).

Rich clown (Fred), Rising Sun,
Indiana, 1985 (Franzen
Brothers).

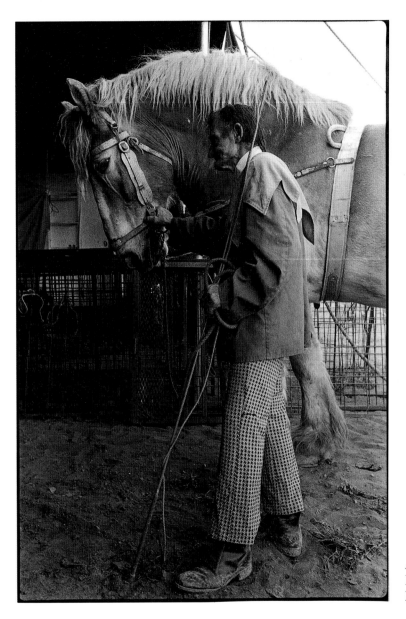

Alfonso and Chulo, Window
Rock, Arizona, 1984 (Carson &
Barnes).

Levitation (Lili), Palestine,
Illinois, 1985 (Carson &
Barnes).

Calliope (The Great Circus
Parade), Milwaukee, Wisconsin,
1986.

Backyard wash, Barstow,
California, 1984 (Carson &
Barnes).

Ringmaster (Bill), Tell City,
Indiana, 1985 (Franzen
Brothers).

Strange animals, New
Brunswick, New Jersey, 1986
(Toby Tyler).

Watching setup—Amish family,
Salem, Indiana, 1986 (Carson &
Barnes).

Wet clown (Rod), Buena Vista,
Virginia, 1986 (Roberts
Brothers).

Andrea, Milwaukee, Wisconsin,
1986 (Carson & Barnes).

Sunday services (Father Toner),
Brick Town, New Jersey, 1986
(Clyde Beatty–Cole Brothers).

Backyard romance (Jose and
Manuela, et al.), Paulding, Ohio,
1985 (Kelly–Miller Brothers).

Sidewall shadows, Alderson,
West Virginia, 1986 (Roberts
Brothers).

Caged tiger, De Land, Florida, 1986 (Clyde Beatty–Cole Brothers, winter quarters).

Chuck's trailer, Cedar City, Missouri, 1985 (Carson & Barnes).

Small clown (Pete), New
Brunswick, New Jersey, 1986
(Toby Tyler).